C'mon Geeze Yer Patter!

C'mon Geeze Yer Patter!

by Peter Mason

SEANACHAIDH PRESENTATIONS
Port Glasgow, Scotland PA14 5XS.

1987

ISBN:0 948963 30 1

Cover Design and Graphics by:Stephen Kennedy.

Cover Photograph by:Vincent's, Glasgow.

Printed by:Bell & Bain Ltd., Glasgow.

Seanachaidh Publishing,
Unit 44, Block 8, Industrial Estate,
Port Glasgow,
Scotland PA14 5XS.

To ANNA
"A right wee stoater if ever there wis wan."

HOW TO USE THIS BOOK

There are 4 simple ways in which the reader can tackle the contents of **"C'mon Geeze Yer Patter"**:

FIRST: Sit back and read it from cover to cover.

SECOND: Choose sections of particular interest to you from the contents list and work your way through them at your leisure.

THIRD: Use the index at the back to track down words you want to know about.

FOURTH: Find out how good your family and friends are at translating into English what you read out to them.

N.B.   Either way, you'll love it as you laugh and learn.

AUTHOR'S INTRODUCTION

No book on the Glasgow and West of Scotland dialect
can ever be complete. If ever such a book was written, it
would mean the language was dead or, at the very least,
static.
I don't believe that this will ever be the case. On the
contrary, this dialect, affectionately referred to as the
patter, is one of the most colourful and imaginative to be
found anywhere and it is developing with every new
generation.
Possibly, its greatest attractions lie in its humour and the
changing emphasis of words and phrases when found in
a variety of situations.
This book has been written in such a way that everyday
situations can be highlighted and the *patter,* put into
context, can be enjoyed to its fullest.

Peter Mason

CONTENTS

CONTENTS

BASICS FOR THE VISITOR

"NAW HANKS, A'VE JIST EATEN"

I	Ah	"Ah like Glasgow"
I am	A'm	"A'm lost"
I am (reply)	Am Ur	"Am ur as well"
I am not	Am Urny	"Am urny here to gie directions"
Of	A or O'	"Ask the driver o' the bus"
You (singular)	Ye	"Ye don't go that way"
You (plural)	Yous	"Yous have to go this way"
You are	Ye'r/Yous'r	"Ye'r/yous'r going the wrang way"
You are not	Ye/yous urny	"Ye/yous urny going the right way"
Yes	Aye	"Aye, this is Glasgow"
No	Naw	"Naw, this isn't Aberdeen"
No (reply)	Nut	"Nut, it isn't Edinburgh either"
Thank you	Hanks	"Hanks for helping me"
No thank you	Naw hanks	"Naw hanks, I've just eaten"

I don't understand.	"Whit dae ye mean?"
	or "A'm no quite gettin ye!"
	or "Come again?"
Please speak more slowly.	"Gauny slow doon a bit"
Excuse me!	"Hey Jimmy!"
Can you help me?	"Gauny geeze a haun oot"
Can I have...	"Gauny geeze..."
What time is it?	"Hiv ye got the time?"
I must go now.	"Ah hiv tae git gaun"
Go away.	"**** off!"

GREETINGS TO YOU ALL

HULLORRER! IT'S YERSEL THEN!

How's it gaun, auld freen?	And what might life be like with you, my old friend?
Hullorrer. It's yersel' then!	Hello there. I wasn't expecting you!
How're ye getting oan?	How is life treating you!

A BODY IS A BODY

HUMAN BODY (FRONT)

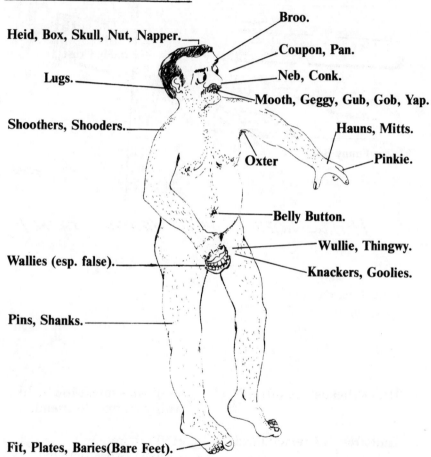

Broo.

Heid, Box, Skull, Nut, Napper.

Coupon, Pan.

Neb, Conk.

Lugs.

Mooth, Geggy, Gub, Gob, Yap.

Shoothers, Shooders.

Hauns, Mitts.

Oxter

Pinkie.

Belly Button.

Wullie, Thingwy.

Wallies (esp. false).

Knackers, Goolies.

Pins, Shanks.

Fit, Plates, Baries(Bare Feet).

4

A BODY IS A BODY

HUMAN BODY (BACK)

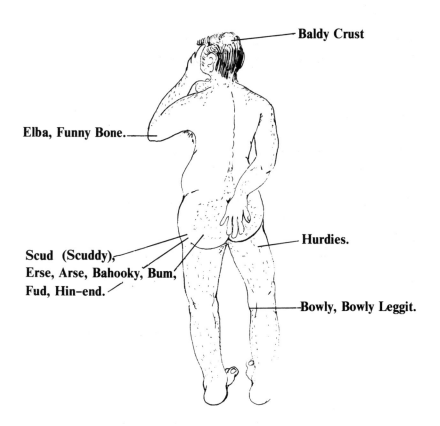

Baldy Crust

Elba, Funny Bone.

Hurdies.

Scud (Scuddy),
Erse, Arse, Bahooky, Bum,
Fud, Hin-end.

Bowly, Bowly Leggit.

5

Where did ye git the Baldy, Tam?
Who gave you the extra-short haircut, Thomas?

Hauns aff! Noo!
Would you please remove your hands from that object
immediately.

Wull ye check big Rab's mental keeker.
Look at the terribly bruised eye Robert has.

John's got lugs oan 'im like a coupla plates.
John's ears are quite large.

A'll no tell ye again, sit oan yer arse.
I command you, for the final time, be seated.

She's got a mooth oan her like the Clyde Tunnel.
She is very loud-mouthed.

Wance mair and ye'r pan's wasted. A'm tellin ye.
I must say that, if you repeat those actions, your face will be
assailed.

He's no quoted 'cos he sheds his hair tae the wrang side.
He has been ostracised because the parting in his hair is too
far to the right.

Ye'r gauny git skelly watchin a' that telly.
You will become cross-eyed if you don't curtail the amount of
time spent as a television viewer.

Yon's a gallus wee tashie ye'v got noo neebur.
I certainly approve of your newly acquired moustache, my
friend.

If ye'r hauns are fu', bung it under ye'r oxter.
If your hands are already laden, place the article high up under your arm.

Pick up Granny's wallies? Nae Danger!
Lay hold of Grandmother's dentures? You have no hope of me doing that.

Ye'll git a skelf fleein aboot in ye'r baries.
You will soon suffer from a splinter if you run around with naked feet.

Yon hammer's nae use, Tam's corrie fisted.
That hammer is inappropriate as Tom is left handed.

Yon wee humphy backit filla fun it in the sheuch.
That small man with the rounded back found it at the kerbside.

She's got a pair a hurdies oan her like Desperate Dan.
She has thighs and hips like Desperate Dan (Comic character).

Ah hope a'm no aboot when that plook goes aff.
I hope I'm not here when your pimple bursts.

How many parts
of the body
do *you* know?

THE WEEKLY WASH

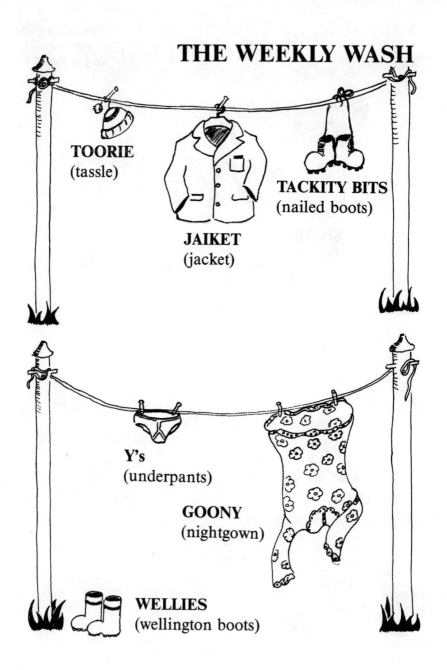

TOORIE
(tassle)

JAIKET
(jacket)

TACKITY BITS
(nailed boots)

Y's
(underpants)

GOONY
(nightgown)

WELLIES
(wellington boots)

THE WEEKLY WASH

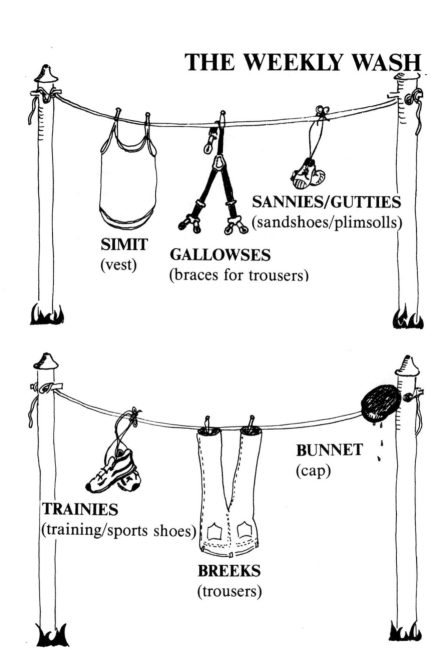

SIMIT
(vest)

GALLOWSES
(braces for trousers)

SANNIES/GUTTIES
(sandshoes/plimsolls)

TRAINIES
(training/sports shoes)

BREEKS
(trousers)

BUNNET
(cap)

How longs that yous
pair hiv been
winchin noo?

COURTSHIP AND MARRIAGE

FANCY GAUN UP THE
PALLY FUR THE JIGGIN?

Ah got a click at the jiggin last night wi' wee Betty.
I managed to persuade Betty to let me escort her home from
the dance yesterday evening.

Ah think ye'r gauny hiv tae ditch that yin. He's nae use.
I suggest you end your relationship with him.
He's not good for you.

C'mon an coorie inty me.
Come and snuggle into me.

Ah wis black affronted gittin a dissy at Boots's coarner.
I was really embarassed when my date didn't show up at our
meeting place in the City Centre.

Fancy gaun up the Pally fur the jiggin?
Would you care to go to the dancehall?

That's yon new laud o' hers fae the Drum.
That's her latest boyfriend from Drumchapel.

Don't ask her furra lumber. Dead certs y'll git a knockback.
Don't ask her to walk home with you.
She will certainly refuse.

Ma man an' me are aye at wan anothers throats.
My husband and I are forever arguing.

When we got merrit, a' the weans came tae the scrammle.
A whole host of children came to our wedding to participate
in the violent free-for-all when the newlyweds scatter money
amongst them.

How long's that yous pair hiv been winchin noo?
How long has your relationship lasted with one another?

**See yon racket yous two make in that close when ye'r winchin,
it's terrible, so it is.**
You make an awful noise as you kiss and cuddle in the
entrance of the building.

If ye think ye merrit me furra skivvy, then ye'r wrang.
If you think my role in this marriage is that of housemaid,
then you are gravely mistaken.

14

LIFE AT HOME

A' THE
FAimiLY
AT HAMĒ.

Ah hate workin yon new fangled waashin' machine.
I hate operating that highly technological washing machine.

There's a fit a stoor oan yon telly.
There's a thick film of dust on the television.

Mind take the hoover tae that oose in ablow the bed.
Remember to vacuum clean the fluff underneath the bed.

Gauny iron the runkles oot ma shurt, maw?
Will you press the creases from my shirt, mother?

Dook yer haun in the waater an see if it's cauld yit.
Plunge your hand into the water and ascertain its
temperature.

A'm aye the wan tae hiv tae kennle the fire.
I always have to kindle the fire

Am fed up reddin up efter yous.
I'm depressed at continually tidying your things away.

Look at they pots. A'm gauny hiv tae steep them.
Those pots are so dirty, they'll have to be soaked.

Don't tim yon tea oot. A'm no done wi' it.
Don't empty out the tea. I'm not yet finished with it.

Ye'll fun clean sheets in the kist.
You'll get clean sheets in the linen chest.

Ye'll need tae let the tea mask a bit mair.
Allow the tea to infuse for a while longer.

That pulley's broke. Git the winter dykes oot.
The drying rail has broken. Bring out the clothes horse.

Ye'll need tae doss doon oan the flair the night.
You will have to sleep on the floor tonight.

16

A' the weans are fur the byne the morra night.
All the children will be having a bath tomorrow night.

Evrybody's oot the back sittin'.
Everyone is sitting outside at the rear of the house.

It's no ma turn fur the close. Ah did it last week.
It's not my turn to wash the entranceway to the tenement. I washed it last week.

Gauny hurry up in that cludgy, a'm near bent double.
Will you please hurry out of the bathroom, I need in urgently.

YE'LL NEED TAE DOSS DOON OAN THE FLAIR THE NIGHT.

The granny blew aff the lum an' landed in the back green.
The cowl blew off the chimney and landed on the lawn at the rear of the house.

Who loaked yon poor cat in the lobby press?
Who locked that poor cat in the hall cupboard?

He lies in yon scratcher of his tae a' hoors.
He remains in bed until late in the day.

YE'R AWFY PEELY WALLY
LOOKIN THE DAY!

IN SICKNESS AND HEALTH

YE BETTER MIND HE DIZNY
SMIT YE WI
THE SNOT!

Tell yer Granny ah wis askin efter her.
Inform your Grandmother that I pass on my best wishes to her.

Everytime ah swally somethin, ah waant tae boke.
Whenever I eat anything, I feel nauseated.

A've hud the skitters fur mair than a week noo.
A've hud the scoots fur mair than a week noo.
I have been suffering from diarrohea for more than a week.

Ye'r awfy peely-wally lookin the day.
You don't look well today.

A'm gauny need a sick line fur the work.
A'm gauny need a panel line fur the work.
My employer requires me to produce a certificate of my illness.

A'm oan the panel furra month wi this gammy leg.
I will be absent from work and collecting state sickness benefit because of my leg injury.

Ah thought it wis a plook but it's turned oot a bile.
I imagined it only to be a small pimple but it has emerged as a boil.

A've no heard Roddy pumpin as much in a' ma days.
Roderick has been breaking wind lately, more than at any other time I can remember.

Moira's hin-end's rid raw wi jookin aboot on yon cuddies.
Moira's buttocks are very sore and inflamed due to her Pony Treking activities.

Ma pinkie's gowpin wi yon big skelf.
My small finger is extremely painful because of the splinter embedded in it.

Ye'v got a real sore wan there.
That really is a painful injury.

Ah WENT OAN MA
NECK AN BROKE
MA LEG.

20

A've been feelin a bit hingy this weather.
I've been rather out of sorts lately.

Ah think a've ta'en the measles aff the wean.
I think I've contracted measles from my child.

A've got tae git a jag in the bum cos that dug but me.
I have to have an injection in the buttocks because I was bitten by a dog.

Ye'll need a photy tae see if its broke.
You require an xray to determine if it is fractured.

Ah racked ma back howkin dockens an that.
I strained my back whilst weeding the garden.

Ye better mind he dizny smit ye wi the snot.
Take care you are not infected with his common cold.

Ma left leg keeps oan gaun tae sleep.
My left leg frequently becomes numb.

Ah staved ma big toe breengin aboot in ma baries.
I sprained my large toe frolicking around in my bare feet.

It's a' right sayin, 'git that doon ye', but ah canny swally it.
I'm sorry but it's not appropriate for me to take that internally, as I have great difficulty swallowing.

Ah went oan ma neck an' broke ma leg.
I fell and fractured a bone in my leg.

There's nae use walkin aboot wi' the snotters blindin ye.
It's pointless being up and about with such a heavy cold.

My! Ye'r in fine fettle the day.
You certainly seem to be in high spirits today.

THE ENTERTAINER

A WEE
ROONY APPLAUSE ?

Ye canny whack yon guid pipe baun fae Kirkie.
You can't do better than the Kirkintilloch pipe band for
entertainment.

A'm gaun ben the room tae hiv a hingy.
I'm going through to the other room to lean out of the
window and converse with passers–by.

Fancy gaun up the toon tae the jiggin the night?
Would you welcome an invitation to go dancing in the City
Centre this evening?

We were knottin oorsels at yon comic.
We were laughing uproariously at the comedian.

Ma mither c'n sing like a lintie when she waants.
My mother can sing like a linnet when she cares to.

D'ye fancy gaun oot oan the randan the morra night?
How would you feel about over-indulging in sensual
pleasures tomorrow evening?

A'm gauny take the weans doon tae the shows.
I will accompany the children to the fairground.

The pictures wur fair stowed oot fur yon wan.
The cinema was extremely well attended for that particular
film.

We're aff oan a sub-crawl furra laugh.
We are now going to ride on the undeground and alight at
every station for an alcoholic drink for the purpose of light
entertainment.

Yon wis a rerr terr, so it wis.
That was an excellent outing, it really was.

Yon magician wis rotten but the singer wis magic.
That magician was terrible but the singer was very good.

A WEE
Wummin
Hivvin A
Hingy
ooty the
Windy.

THE GAMES PEOPLE PLAY

G-AUNY G-EEZA SHOODERY
SO'S Ah C'N SEE ?

Git some chalk furra beds, an' we'll play at peever.
Get some chalk for marking out, and we'll play at hopscotch.

Go'n git yer bladder an' ah'll gie ye a gemme at heiders.
Fetch your leather football and we'll play at heading it to each other.

The gemme's a bogey, sumdy cheated.
That game has to be left unfinished as someone has cheated.

Gauny geeza shoodery so's ah c'n see?
Will you lift me up on your shoulders so that I can get a better view?

Ah broke ma airm when ah fell aff yon daft chute.
I fractured my arm when I fell from the playground slide.

Gauny geeze a coal cairry up yon hill?
Will you give me a piggy back up this hill?

If ye don't go het, ye'r no playin'.
If you don't take on the role of catcher, you won't be able to participate.

Ma wee pal c'n dive aff the tap dale at the baths.
My little friend can dive from the highest diving board at the swimming pool.

That's got tae be a stoat–up ref.
In all fairness, surely you must bounce the ball between the opposing players to restart the game, referee.

Ah don't waanty play at peever, a waanty play at tig.
I don't wish to play hopscotch, I'd rather play at tag
(the chasing game).

Haw da! Gauny geeza birly?
Excuse me father! Will you pick me up and spin me around?

Don't play at bools wi' him, he's a wee cheater!
Don't play at marbles with him, he cheats!

Ah caw'd ma peerie too hard an' it went fleein' through a windy.
I struck my spinning top overzealously and it went through a window.

Ye'r no meant tae plunk they bools as hard as a' that.
One is not supposed to eject the marbles quite so vigorously.

The wean's ben the scullery skiddlin in the sink.
The child is through the kitchen playing with water in the sink.

Ye could make the liddy yon tin can inty a rerr skiter.
The lid of that cannister would make a very good flying object.

C'mon we'll grab a hudgie oan yon big van.
Let's hang onto the back of that big van when it's moving.

Gaun lets see ye daein a wee dokey.
Let's see you doing a forward roll.

Ah c'n tummle ma wulkies twinty times withoot stoapin.
I can do twenty forward rolls non-stop.

Ah DON'T
WANTY PLAY
AT PEEVER.
Ah WANTY
PLAY AT
TIG!

27

LET'S GO SHOPPING

Humphin
Messages
Hame Fae
Doon The
Toon.

2 punna aipples.	.90 kilos of apples.
Hauf-a-dizzen tattie scones.	6 potato scones.
A jaur a clappy doos.	A jar of black mussels.
2 boatles a ginger.	2 bottles of aerated water.
A punna mince.	.22 kilograms of minced beef.
2 punna square slice.	.90 kilograms of square–cut sausage meat.
A cludgy roll.	1 toilet tissue.
A purn a threed.	1 reel of cotton.
Pkt. kirby grips.	A packet of hair pins.
A 5-pun bag a tatties.	A 2.2 kilogram bag of potatoes.
3 nice haddies.	3 fresh pieces of haddock.
A pink dummy tit.	A pink, rubber teat for baby to suck on soothingly.
A sneck furra back door.	Lock/bolt for the rear entrance to the house.
Wanny them gallus Glesca phrase books.	A copy of "C'mon Geeze Yer Patter!"
A paper.	A copy of the usual daily newspaper.

LET'S GO SHOPPING

GAUNY GEEZE 2 BOATLES A L.D. MISSES ?

Messages fae the cairry-oot section.

2 boatles a L.D.

A boatle a Lanny.
A dizzen cans a heavy.
Hauf-a-dizzen cans a light.
A hauf boatle a voddy.
A wee boatle a pep.

Drinks list from the off-licence.

2 bottles of 'El Dorado' wine.
1 bottle of 'Lanliq' wine.
12 tins of best bitter.
6 tins of best mild beer.
A half bottle of vodka.
A small bottle of peppermint cordial.

~MENU~
furra Motta

STARTERS

Scotch Broth   Soup with barley added.

Ginger   Aerated water

FISH COURSE

Arbroath Smokies   Smoked Haddock

Wulks   Whelks.

Clappy Doos   Mussels.

Haddies   Haddock.

MAIN COURSE

Fry ups   Mixed Grill.

Tatties and mince   Potatoes and minced beef.

Haggis and neeps   Haggis and turnip

Square slice and chips   Sliced sausage and chips.

Tattie scones and eggs   Potato scones and eggs.

SWEETS

Aipples   Apples.

Icies   Various Ice Creams.

Pokey Hats   Ice cream in a wafer cone.

EATING

SNACKS

Jeely Pieces	Jam sandwiches
(pan or plain breid)	(either of 2 popular breads)
Hot Pea Specials	Hot peas in vinegar.
Bylt eggs an' toast	Boiled eggs with toasted bread.

CAIRRY OOTS

Single Fish	Fried fish on its own.
Fish Supper	Fried fish with chips.
Single Haggis	Haggis in batter on its own.
Haggis Supper	Haggis in batter with chips.
Single Sausage	2 Sausages fried in batter.
Sausage Supper	2 Sausages fried in batter with chips.

USEFUL PHRASES TO KNOW AND UNDERSTAND.

Gauny geeze an aipple tae chow oan?
May I have an apple to nibble?

Whit'll ah dae wi' this stump?
What shall I do with this apple core?

Ye must be starvin the wye ye'r gittin horsed inty that.
Ye must be starvin the wye ye'r gittin beasted inty that.
You must be very hungry the way you're eating so hurriedly.

Gauny make ma piece an ootsider.
Will you make my sandwich from the thick, outside slices of the bread.

A've jist swallied a bone ooty yon haddy.
I've just swallowed a fish bone.

Git that doon ye an' ye'll grou big.
Eat your meal and you'll become big and strong.

C'n we git another ashet a thae chips?
May we have another tray of chips?

A've ta'en a scunnering tae fish efter the last time.
I'm not at all happy about eating fish after having a bad experience with it.

There's nae need tae gollop it, ye gutsy thing ye.
You don't have to rush your food, you greedy person.

Ah waant lashins a gravy oan ma pie.
I would like a lot of gravy on my pie.

Ye'r an awfy pick when it comes tae food.
You don't really eat very much.

Ah'll jist pit this in a poke an take it hame tae the dug.
I'll put this in a paper bag and take it home for my dog.

If ye didny slurp s'much, ye widny slitter.
If you didn't try to inhale your food noisily, you wouldn't drip it down your chin and clothing.

A'm right stapped efter that.
I've had quite sufficient.

Yon mulk's definately turned.
That milk had definitely gone sour.

Ah c'd eat a scabby dug, so ah could.
Ah c'd eat a scabby horse, so ah could.
I really am very hungry.

THIS'S A RIGHT HIGH FALUTIN PLACE.

Ye'd think they'd sine oot the plates afore dishin up yer dinner.
They should rinse the plates before serving our meal on them.

They cups c'd dae wi a wee steep.
Those cups could do with being soaked in hot water.

Ah ony take a wee toty tate a mulk in ma tea.
I only take a small amount of milk in my tea.

This is a right high falutin place this.
This is a very posh establishment.

There's a big dawd a fat oan this.
There's a rather large lump of fat on this.

Yon Efter 8's they dished up wur definately fuisted.
Those after-dinner-mints we were served were slightly
mouldy.

DRINKING

HE C'D TAKE
A FAIR
WEE BUCKET,
So HE COULD.

S'ma bell. Whit'r ye fur?
It's my turn to purchase drinks for us all. What would you
care to order?

C'mon w'll jist hiv a kitty furra bevvy.
Let us pool some of our finances for the purpose of
purchasing alcohol.

Ah see the auld man wis oan a bender last night.
I notice my father was out drinking heavily yesterday evening.

Fancy a dauner tae the offie furra cairry-oot?
Shall we walk to the off-licence and purchase some alcohol?

Ah c'd fair dae wi' a lager fur this drooth a've got.
I wish I could have a pint of lager to quench my thirst.

Jeeze oh! Whit a session that ended up.
I declare! The outcome of that social gathering was beyond
my initial expectations.

He was *slightly* intoxicated with alcoholic beverage.
He wis a wee bit tipsy.
He wis well on.
He wis hauf steamin.
He wis hauf fu'.
He hud a fair bucket.

He was *extremely* intoxicated with alcoholic beverage.
He wis bevvied.
He wis blootered.
He wis oot h's brain.
He wis fleein.
He wis fu'.
He wis guttered.
He wis mirauculus.
He wis paralitic.
He wis steamboats.
He wis right steamin.
He wis stotious.
He wis roarin.
He wis high as a kite.
He wis stoned oot h's box.
He wis as fu' as a wulk.

36

A typical order from a social gathering of 3 – 5 persons may sound something like the following:

Ah'll hiv a hauf an a hauf.
My order is a half pint of beer and a small glass of whisky.

Mines's a heavy.
A pint of best bitter for me.

C'n ah git a wee nippy sweetie?
May I have a small glass of whisky?

A screwtap'll dae fur me. By the neck, by the way.
A bottle of beer with a screw-off top will suit me fine.
Incidently, I'll pour it myself.

Jist geeza voddy.
Just supply me with a glass of vodka.

Ah'll hiv the same.
I will take all of the above.
(usually from a would-be wit)

A HAUF
AN'
A HAUF,

Gauny geeza sluggy yer skoosh fur ma mooth.
May I have a sip of your aerated water to combat the bad taste I have in my mouth.

Ah think a'm gauny need a hair o' the dug, cos ma heid's birlin efter last night.
For medical purposes, I may need to consume some more of what I had yesterday evening as my head is spinning.

Gauny stoap that rammy. Ma poor heid's goupin.
Will you stop making a noise. My head is very painful.

Aunty Mary c'n fairly doon a queer bucket, so she kin.
Aunt Mary can certainly consume large quantities of alcohol.

Did ah enjoy masel?
I can't remember a thing about last night.

Ah ended up buyin drink fur the hale jing bang lot.
I finally had to buy the drinks for everyone.

He asked furra slug, then he guzzled it a'.
He asked for a small drink then, greedily, he drank the whole lot.

OUT AND ABOUT

FANCY A TRIP TAE SEE A'
YON NEW FLOOER BEDS
IN GLESCA?

He's got a months hoaliday at the BAR-L.
He's being incarcerated in Barlinie Prison for 30 days.

A'm gaun doon the BARRAS fur some pressies.
I'm going to Glasgow's famous market to purchase some gifts.

It wisnae me ye saw in Blythswood Square.
I deny I was looking for a prostitute at the normal rendezvous point.

Right. Boots Corner, 7'a'clock, Setterday night.
I will meet you at the entrance to Boots department store at 7 o'clock on Saturday evening.

Ah'll git ye in ablow the Hielandman's Umbarella later on.
I'll meet you later under the big Central Station railway bridge
in Argyle Street.

The weans'r oot huntin doon lucky middens.
The weans'r oot midgie rakin'.
The kids are off in search of expensive items other people
have discarded in their dustbins.

Ma Granny stays in a wee single–end ahint Shawfield dug track.
My Grandmother lives in a small room and kitchen to
the rear of Shawfield Stadium.

Ah drapped that 10 bob bit an' it rolled doon a stank.
I dropped the 50 pence piece and it rolled down the drain
in the street.

**He wis wheeched away tae the Suffering General wi' his leg
broke.**
He was taken hurriedly to the Southern General Hospital
when he fractured his leg.

We're aff tae the Sarry Heid furra coupla jugs.
We are off to the Saracen's Head public house for a few
drinks.

Ah'll hiv tae go tae the hole in the wa' afore we hit the boozer.
I must go to the Bank's cash dispenser before we reach the
public house.

**The waasher's oot the gemme; ah'll hiv tae go roon tae
the steamie.**
The washing machine has broken down; I'll have to visit
the public laundry.

Ah belang tae the Drum but ma da comes fae Rossy.
I live in Drumchapel but my father originates from Rothesay.

Fancy a trip tae see a' yon new flooer beds in Gleska.
Would you care to go on a visit to the Glasgow Garden
Festival.

WHO hoAKED
THAT pooR CAT
iN THE
LOBBY PRESS ?

A'm no lumberin her a' the wye tae the Briggs.
I'm not escorting her home all the way to Bishopbriggs.

Ah spotted the auld man daunerin doon tae the doocot.
I saw my dad walking aimlessly towards the pidgeon loft.

Ma sister's gaun tae the Dough School efter the hoalidays.
My sister will become a student at Queens College (Domestic
Science) after summer recess.

IT WIS YON
BIG EEJIT THAT
PIT ME UP TAE IT.

LAW AND ORDER

Aye or Naw?
And naney yer wafflin!

It wis yon wee clype owr there that pit the finger oan me.
It was that diminutive informant over yonder whose statement
led to my arrest.

Gie the Polis a haun! Gie yersel a hammerin.
Assist the Police! Beat yourself up!

**Ah done a wan–night lie–in doon the slammer efter that bevvy
session.**
I spent one night in jail following my over–indulgence with
alcohol.

He wis huckled wi' the Polis fur hingin aboot.
He was taken away by the Police for loitering.

It wis him that nocked it; he needs the jile furrit.
It was he who stole it; he deserves a jail sentence for his
crime.

Wisnae me! It's a fit–up.
I did not commit the offence! The charge is a conspiracy
against me.

Ah clocked him pauchlin' they pincils fae the shoap.
I witnessed him stealing the pencils from the shop.

It wis yon big eejit that pit me up tae it.
It was that idiot who encouraged me to do it.

A'm gauny plank yon stuff we snaffled doon in the dunny.
I'm going to hide the goods we stole down in the cellar.

Aye or Naw; and naney yer wafflin.
Yes or No; we don't require an extended explanation.

Right yous lot. Oan yer bikes.
Would you all care to move along please.

Ah hid nuhin tae dae wi' it.
I'm totally innocent.

A THREAT OR A CHALLENGE

Don't act it wi' me you. Right?
You shouldn't push your luck with me. Understand?

A'm jist gauny chin him aboot this rotten bevvy.
I am going to complain to him about this unsatisfactory
drink.

See you, ya bam, ye'r claimed.
I am speaking to you, you idiot, and I am giving you notice
that I intend to be violent towards you.

Come ahead, ya mug ye.
If you want to fight me, you idiot, proceed.

It's gauny be the jile fur you, wee man.
You are very likely to be imprisoned.

Ye better no mess wi' him, by the way.
I strongly advise you against becoming involved with him in any unfriendly manner.

A'm no gauny tell you again, right?
This is your final warning, do you understand?

You got a wee problem, pal?
Do you have a complaint you would like me to respond to?

Whit?...Aye, that *wull* be right.
Pardon?...Well, I dismiss such claims.

Ah'll fix him right away.
I will alter his opinions/actions immediately.

Ye'r mammy'll go through ye when she funs oot whit ye'v done.
Your mother will severely reprimand you when she has knowledge of your deeds.

Ye'r cruisin furra bruisin'.
Your actions are sufficient to attract a violent response.

Ah don't waant any yer snash, right?
I do not wish to hear any impertinent retorts, understand?

Wanst mair an' a'm gauny go right ahead.
Repeat your actions once again and I'll become extremely violent.

Jist draw 'im a sinker, that'll dae it.
You merely have to glower at him to achieve the desired affect.

Don't think a'm feart tae stick up tae you.
Do not assume that I have any fear of accepting your challenge.

Whit is it wi' you anywye?
Please explain why you are acting the way you are.

Whit d'ye think ye'r gawkin' at?
I don't care for the way you keep staring at me.

See if ah hiv tae check you again, ye'r furrit.
If I have to chastise you once more, you'll be in trouble.

Sweeties? Ah'll gie ye sweeties, so a wull.
Confectionery? It'll be something other than confectionery you'll be getting.

Ye better no start tryin tae mix it wi' me.
I suggest you don't get into a heated argument with me.

Right yous, lee 'im alane.
Attention all of you. Let him be in peace.

Ye'r da'll flite oan ye fur brekkin that.
Your father will scold you for breaking that.

YE BETTER No MESS wi HIm,
BY THE WAY!

THERE WIS
A RIGHT
STOOSHIE
EFTER HE
STIFFENED
HIM !

LAYING ON OF HANDS

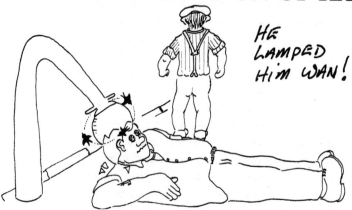

HE LAMPED HIM WAN!

There wis ructions efter he pit the boot in.
There was a brawl after he kicked him.

He got a right sore wan efter gittin' but oan the leg.
He had a nasty wound after being bitten on the leg.

He jist sallied up an' ca'd the legs oot fae ablow him.
He casually approached and swept his legs from beneath him.

The bampot ripped him wi' a chib efter gittin' heidered.
The idiot slashed him with a bladed weapon after being butted.

He wis waantin' hauners but evrybody crapped ooty it.
He required assistance but everyone was too scared to become involved.

There wis a right rammy when the teams went mental.
There was a riot when the two opposing gangs began to fight.

He took the boot right aff his heid.
He kicked him on the head.

There was riotous behaviour after he hit him hard
(on the face?).
There wis a right stooshie efter he banjoed him.
There wis a right stooshie efter he blootered him.
There wis a right stooshie efter he butted him wan.
There wis a right stooshie efter he burst him.
There wis a right stooshie efter he gubbed him.
There wis a right stooshie efter he hung wan oan him.
There wis a right stooshie efter he hut him.
There wis a right stooshie efter he lamped him wan.
There wis a right stooshie efter he scudded him.
There wis a right stooshie efter he stiffened him.
There wis a right stooshie efter he clowted him.
There wis a right stooshie efter he skelped him wan.
There wis a right stooshie efter he skited him.
There wis a right stooshie efter he wannered him wan.
There wis a right stooshie efter he said, "stitch that."
There wis a right stooshie efter he rattled him wan.

They became embroiled in fierce hand–to–hand combat.
The two of them went right ahead.
The two of them got beasted intae wan another.
The two of them got right intae each other's heid.
The two of them got steamed right in.
The two of them got tore in aboot it.

He was soundly defeated.
He got cuffed.
He got wasted.
He got a right kickin'.
He got a real tankin'.
He got a leatherin'.
He got a right meltin'.
He got mollocated.

JUST HOW I FEEL

Ah wis crappin masel oan the backy yon motorbike!

Ah got a right riddy when ah wis fun oot.
Ah got a big beamer when ah wis fun oot.
I was really blushing when I was caught.

Ah wis mortified when the polis came tae the door.
Ah wis black affronted when the polis came tae the door.
I was very embarassed when the policeman came to the house.

Ma mither wis beelin when the auld man came hame paralitic.
My mother was very angry when my father came home drunk.

Ah jist felt like hivvin a wee bubble tae masel.
I just felt like being on my own and quietly weeping

Ah wis crappin masel oan the backy yon moterbike.
I was really frightened as a passenger on that motorcycle.

Sh'll fair go her dinger when she funs oot ye've broke it.
She'll be very angry when she discovers you've broken it.

These crisps don't hauf make you droothy.
These potato snacks really make one thirsty.

A'm gettin intae a right fankle tryin tae wire this plug.
I'm experiencing all sorts of problems trying to wire this plug.

A'm fur gaun tae the pictures.
I'm keen to visit the cinema.

HE ONLY DIS
iT WHEN iT
COMES UP
His HUMPH.

Ah c'd fair go anither wee cuppa tea.
I'd really welcome another small cup of tea.

Ah c'd jist hiv sat doon an' gret.
I felt like sitting down and weeping.

A'm really jist heart roasted wi' the lotty yous.
I'm exasperated with all of you.

Ah hink it's a cracker.
I think it is very good indeed.

He only dis it when it comes up his humph.
He will only do it when he feels in the mood.

A'm right scunnered wi' this rain a' the time.
I'm very irritated with this persistent rainfall.

Ah wis switherin' whether tae go or no.
I find it difficult to decide whether to go or stay.

The last thing ah need's fur you tae geeze yer worries.
The worst scenario, for me, would be for you to start listing
your problems.

Never mind the petted lip; yer no gaun oot.
It's pointless sulking; you're not leaving the house.

Ye'r no gaun oot wi me wi yer face trippin ye.
You won't be going with me if you continue to sulk.

Gauny git a grip oan yersel; ye'r like a fart in a trance.
Please pull yourself together; you seem to be in a dreamworld.

See that yin? He'd gie onybody the grue.
Him? He would make anyone cringe.

A'm nae mair than eechy-ochy aboot watchin telly.
I'm no more bothered about watching television than not
watching it.

Yon scary pictures gie me the heeby-jeebies.
Those horror movies make me shudder.

A'm intae her wi the rid dress oan.
I'm attracted to the girl in the red dress.

A'm s' knackered ah couldny walk the lengthy masel.
I'm so weary I don't feel like moving.

Mibby ah might, but there again, mibby ah wullny.
I may, but conversely, I may not.

A'm fair missin the sweeties wi this diet.
I certainly miss having confectionery because of my diet.

Ma heid's nippin wi' a' this talk aboot flooers.
I can't take any more of this incessant talk about flowers.

Ah aye loss the rag wi' a' these traffic lights.
I constantly lose patience with all of these traffic lights.

Ye'r jist feelin miffed cause ye wullny get.
You are just upset because you won't be able to attend.

Ah really feel sick aboot the hale thing.
I'm very upset about the whole affair.

It's a thought hivvin tae git up at that time in the mornins.
I'm not looking forward to rising so early in the mornings.

The wean's as high as a kite aboot startin school the morra.
The child is very excited about going to school for the first time tomorrow.

A'm no gaun; a'm oot the gemme.
A'm no gaun; a'm knacked.
A'm no gaun; a'm jiggered.
I'm not going, as I'm extremely weary.

I DECLARE!

Ya bandit! Ah jist skelped ma funny bone aff yon palin.
You !XXXX! I've accidently hit my elbow against a fence post.

Aw naw! That's that telly away again.
I don't believe it! The television has just broken down once
more.

Ooyah! That thing jist wannered me oan the heid.
!XXXX! That missile hit me on the head.

Ya beautyyyyyy!
Perfectly wonderful!

C'mon, geeze a boady at least, wull ye!
If you cannot manage to win the game, liven it up with some
unsportsmanlike play!

Aw the shame!
Oh dear, you have my sympathy.

Nae tother a ba' tae me!
This will not cause me any problems whatsoever.

Yeeeeess!
This is completely in line with my hopes.

Aw the nice! Whit age is the wean noo?
How delightful! How old is the child now.

Hell mend ye! Ah warnt ye umpteen times tae stay aff the railway.
You deserve what you got! I warned you on many occasions not to go onto the railway.

Sufferin duck! That's twiced ye've couped ma heavy.
!XXXX! That is the second occassion on which you've overturned my glass of beer.

Dead certs, so it is!
Absolutely certain!

Git tore inty them! Ye'll skoosh it!
Participate enthusiastically! You will win easily!

C'mon, move yersel!
Accompany me at a slightly quicker pace!

A'm aff! This place is right boggin.
I'm leaving! I really don't like this place.

Whit a guff! Wis that you?
What an obnoxious smell! Are you responsible?

Ya hoachy pig!
You have much more than your fair share of luck.

Come away, Scotland!
Try not to lose again, Scotland!

Nae danger!
An absolute certainty.

Aw dearie me!
Is that so!

Aw jeeze oh! If ah'd clocked it ah widny hiv stepped oan it.
!XXXX! If I had noticed it, I would not have trod on it!

Hey Jimmy, got chyngey a ten bob bit?
Excuse me sir, do you have change of a fifty pence coin?

Gen up, ah didny mean it, mister.
Honestly, I did not intend to do that, sir!

Gaun yersel! Ah aye kent ye hud it in ye.
Continue! I always knew you were capable.

We arra peepel!
We really are doing well, for once.

WHIT A GUFF! WIS THAT YOU?

That's the gemme! Wance mair and ye'll hiv it.
That's the correct method! One more practice run and you'll
have mastered it.

Git a grip oan yersel you. Wull ye!
Will you try to control yourself. Please.

Hullooooo!
This is what I've been eagerly awaiting.

Git inty them! A've pyed good money fur this.
Be more competitive. I have paid handsomely and expect a
better perfomance.

Aw, how no?
Why not?

I RESENT THAT REMARK

That's a right wan tae talk.
He is no better than those he chooses to criticise.

Ye'r no winchin that wee toley urye?
Surely you're not courting that little piece of excrement?

A've no seen such a glaiket lookin sowl in a' ma days.
I have never seen such a stupid looking person.

You mibby think he's somethin, but ah think he's hacket.
You may think he is quite alright, but I think he's ugly.

That wee yin fae the Briggs c'n be a right wee neb at times.
The little one from Bishopbriggs can sometimes be quite nosey.

Ah mind him. Whit a scunner.
Ah mind him. Whit a nyaff.
I remember him. Very unappealing indeed.

He jist disny hiv the gumshin furrit.
He really doesn't have the necessary intelligence.

Yon Toon Cooncil couldny run a menage.
The District Council couldn't organise the simplest of things.

Don't let that wee smout boss ye aboot.
Don't allow such a small person to give you orders.

Yon yins worse than a man short, so he is.
We'd be better off with no one than we would be with him.

A've no come across sumdy as donnert as him.
I've never met anyone so stupid.

Don't listen tae him, he's nuthin but a patter merchant.
Ignore him, he just loves to hear himself talk.

He's awa' wi' the fairies.
He is an idiot.(or) He lives in a world of dreams.

Beware! He is rather unbalanced and likely to act crazily.
Watch it! he's a right bampot.
Watch it! he's a right heidbanger.
Watch it! he's a right heidcase.
Watch it! he's a right heid the ba'.
Watch it! he's a right bear.
Watch it! he's a right nutter.
Watch it! he's a right maddy.
Watch it! he's a right mental case.

He is a coward.
He's a crapper.
He's a crapbag.
He's a big fearty.
He's a big jessie.

Her chastity or faithfulness is suspect.
She's nuthin but a bun.
She's nuthin but a dyke.
She's nuthin but a hairy.
She's nuthin but a slag.

You are no more than an idiot.
Ye'r nuthin but an eejit!
Ye'r nuthin but a bam!
Ye'r nuthin but a bampot!
Ye'r nuthin but a dooly!
Ye'r nuthin but a doowally!
Ye'r nuthin but a tube!
Ye'r nuthin but a dooby!
Ye'r nuthin but a dough heid!
Ye'r nuthin but a tumshie!
Yer heids fulla broken boattles.
Yer heids fulla mince.
Yer jist no the fuul shullin'.

COULD BE FLATTERY

I think that was terrific.
Ah think yon wis dead brill.
Ah think yon wis gallus.
Ah think yon wis rerr.
Ah think yon wis spot oan.
Ah think yon wis magic.

OOR PETE'S A
DAB HAUN AT
FLINGIN PAIRTIES

Yon lassie next door's a right wee honey.
Yon lassie next door's a right wee stoater.
Yon lassie next door's a right wee brammer.
The girl who lives next door to me is very attractive.

Yon goalie played a stormer the second hauf.
That goalkeeper played exceptionally well in the second part
of the game.

Oor Pete's a dab haun at flingin pairties.
Peter is very skilled at organising parties.

Ye hiv tae be well–quoted tae get aff wi' her.
You have to be highly thought of, if you are to have a chance
of courting her.

? ? ? ? ? ? ? ? ? ?

? ? ? ? ? ? ? ? ? ?

? ? ? ? ? ? ? ? ? ?

? ? ? ? ? ? ? ? ? ?

? ? ? ? ? ? ? ? ? ?

? ? ? ? ? ? ? ? ? ?

? ? ? ? ? ? ? ? ?

? ? ? ? ? ? ? ? ?

IS THAT WHAT IT MEANS?

*A'm No Sittin wi Him,
cos He's Honkin.*

It's that cauld oot there, a'm chitterin.
It's so cold outside, I'm shivering uncontrollably.

A'm no sittin wi' him, cos he's honkin.
I'm not sitting beside him because of his body odour.

Don't bother yer shurt.
Don't even think about such a thing.

Gauny geeza swatchy at yer paper, pal?
May I have a look at your newspaper?

Ah didny run ooty petrol, the thing jist clapped oot oan me.
I didn't run out of petrol, the car just broke down completely.

Right yous, nae cairry-oan, by the way.
Remember now, no getting into trouble.

A've got nuthin but a pocket fu' a smash.
I have nothing but small change in my pocket.

Yon pictures hingin squinty.
That painting is hanging askew.

Onybuddy seen ma thingumygig?
Has anyone seen my........?

Ye better take yer brolly cos it's gauny plump.
You should take your umbrella as it is going to rain heavily.

Ye'll need an appointment tae see the big high heid yin.
Ye'll need an appointment tae see the heid bummer.
You'll have to have an appointment if you want an interview
with the 'man at the top'.

This book's pure hoachin wi' gallus Gleska patter.
This publication if full of great examples of the Glasgow
language.

66

That'll be the cup up the air; the big yins injurt.
We now have little chance of winning the trophy; our main
player has suffered an injury.

Ye'r nuthin but a big sook, so ye ur.
You are no more than a 'yes man'.

Ye look a right ticket in they auld claes, so ye dae.
You certainly look a mess in those old clothes.

C'n ye no stoap yer moochin for a meenit?
Are you unable to refrain from scrounging even temporarily?

Every time ah ask him summat, he throws me a deefy.
Whenever I ask him anything, he ignores me.

I don't believe you.
Pull the other wan, its got bells oan it.
Don't gie me a' that patter.
D'ye think ah came up the Clyde oan a bike.
D'ye think ah came up the Clyde oan a banana boat.

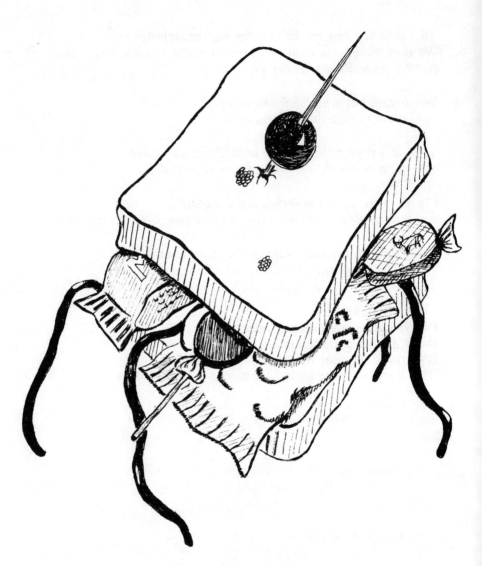

AH HUD SWEETIES AN GINGER
FUR MA PLAYPIECE.

THAT'LL TEACH YOU

C'MON WE'LL JIST DOG IT THE DAY AN' GO FURRA DAUNER.

Ma maw aye telt me tae stick in at school.
My mother always advised me to study enthusiastically when at school.

Auld 'Baldy Bain', the heidie, huckled me fur hingin' aboot.
Our elderly, bald-headed head teacher, reprimanded me for loitering.

Oor beak's dead crabbit wi' us a'.
Our headmaster is very short-tempered with the pupils.

The food at oor dinner school's aye mince.
The food at our school's cafeteria is never to my liking.

Ah hud sweeties an ginger fur ma playpiece.
I had confectionary and aerated water for my snack at school.

69

Ah got 3 of the belt fur cheatin'.
Ah got 3 of the tawse fur cheatin'.
I was given 3 strokes with a leather thong for conferring with another pupil.

He ony got a hunner lines cos the belt's oot the gemme noo.
He received a repetitive writing penalty as corporal punishment is no longer used.

C'mon w'll jist dog it the day an go furra dauner.
Let us play truant today and go for a walk.

A'm gauny hiv tae haun in a note cos ah wis aff.
I will have to submit a written explanation for my absence.

If ye plunk it, the school board'll git ye an yer ma an da's fur the jile.
If you play truant, the education authorites will find out and your parents could face legal action.

Ah never did git the hang of yon big gizinties at school.
I was never able to cope with long division at school.

IN AND OUT OF WORK

Ah got ma books fae the work last week.
Ah got the bag fae the work last week.
Ah got ma jotters fae the work last week.
My employment was terminated last week.

A'm gauny hiv tae sign oan doon the buroo the morra.
I have to register at the employment bureau tomorrow.

Ah'll see ye ootside the work when ye louse.
I'll meet you outside the factory when you finish work.

A've pit in furra joab wi' the Corpie.
I've made application for a position with Glasgow District
Council.

They laid me aff efter a month jist.
They terminated my employment after only a month had
passed.

A've got anither homer tae dae the night.
I'm doing paid work in my own time this evening.

**Mind that joab ah pit in fur wi' the Corpie? Well, ah got a knock
back.**
Do you remember the position I applied for with Glasgow
District Council? Well, my application was unsuccessful.

A'm oan the sick. Here's ma sick line.
A'm oan the panel. Here's ma panel line.
I am officially ill. Here is my medical certificate.

A SHOVEL ENGINEER
(Labourer)

A SWEATY
(P.E. Teacher)

A POLIS
(Policeman)

CHANTY WRASTLER
A LAVVY DIVER
(Plumber)

A CLIPPIE
(Bus Conductress)

A MIDGIE MAN
(Refuse Collector)

A JANNY
(Janitor)

A JINER
(Carpenter)

A HEIDIE
(Head Teacher)

A PARKY
(Park Ranger)

A TATTIE HOWKER
(Potato Picker)

IN THE NICK OF TIME

GIT TAE BED,
YE'R UP EARLY THE MORNS MORN.

Ye'r no gettin sweeties. Ye'r jist efter yer tea.
You are not being supplied with confectionery because you
have not long finished your evening meal.

Ah think she's jist aboot ages wi' masel.
I think she is approximately the same age as I am.

Whit time dae ye ca' this? Yer tea's a' by.
Do you realise what time it is? You are late for your evening
meal.

Ah wanst heard the Jags verneer won.
Sometime in the past, someone informed me that Partick
Thistle F.C. almost won.

This'll ony take a wee minute.
I'll have this finished in a very short time.

Git tae bed, ye'r up early the morn's morn.
Go to bed now, as you have to rise early tomorrow
morning.

Urye gauny git a move oan. It's gauny bucket doon.
Will you please hurry before it begins to rain.

Ah mind when a wis at school in Gleska.
I remember when I attended school in Glasgow.

Jeeze oh! Is that you here already?
I declare! You have arrived early.

The auld eejit didny git hame tae yon time.
The old fool returned home very late.

Ah'll meet ye jist ootside the work at lousin time.
I will meet you outside the factory when my working day is at
an end.

**A'm gaun tae the pictures the night, but a'm stayin' in the morra
night.**
I'm going to the cinema this evening, but I will remain at
home tomorrow evening.

**If we don't get doon there like the clappers, we'll have long
enough tae wait in yon queue.**
If we don't hurry we will have to queue for an extended length
of time.

Jist bide yer time an' it'll a' work oot.
Be patient and the situation will resolve itself.

Yon nock's stoaped. It needs rowed up.
That clock has stopped. It requires to be wound.

Whit are ye dae'n furra livin this weather?
What is your current occupation?

Is it no aboot time yous two were gittin merrit.
Do you not think you should be setting a date for your
wedding soon.

He's been wi' the Corpie since nineteen–canteen.
He has been employed by Glasgow District Council for a very
long time.

A'm gaun tae the doctors wi' this bad leg the morra.
I have an appointment with the doctor tomorrow
morning because of my injured leg.

Yon train wis majic. We were ooty Embra in a jiffy.
That train was very good. We were out of Edinburgh very
quickly.

Yon nock's bammy!
That clock is not showing the correct time!

Ah hivny been up the Heelands fur yonks.
Ah hivny been up the Heelands furra wheena years.
I haven't visited the Highlands for many years.

GAUNY SHOOT
DOON TAE THE
PAPERSHOAP AN'
GIT ME FAGS?

MOVING AROUND

Ah FANCIED FLITTIN TAE THE BRIGGS
BUT WE'R GAUNY FLIT
TAE THE DRUM INSTEED.

We're aff fur the Fair Fortnight oan an airyplane the morra mornin.
We are off for the two weeks of the Glasgow holiday by plane in the morning.

Ah don't b'lang tae here. Ah come fae Airdrie, and he styes in Rossy.
I am not a native of this place. I reside in Airdrie, and he lives in Rothesay.

Yon caur came fleein roon the ben an' skelped that poor dug.
That automobile sped round the corner and collided with that unfortunate canine.

A'm jist away furra dauner tae the bus comes.
I am off to wander aimlessly until the bus arrives.

Ah fancied flittin tae the Briggs, but we're gauny flit tae the Drum insteed.
I wanted to go and live in Bishopbriggs but we are moving to Drumchapel instead.

Ah wis gaun doon the road oan ma bike when a lorry passed me gaun like the clappers.
I was cycling along the street when a truck overtook me at high speed.

Evrybody's gaun Doon the Watter the morra but a'm no gauny get.
Everyone is taking a boat trip on the River Clyde tomorrow but, unfortunately, I won't be able to accompany them.

Ah canny go a bike.
I am unable to ride a bicycle.

The buses are aff an' ah hud tae humph a' this fae the Central.
The buses are not operating and I had to carry all of these from Glasgow Central Railway Station.

A dauner doon the toon? Ah couldny walk the length of masel.
A leisurely stroll into the City Centre? I couldn't manage to walk anywhere near that distance.

Ah'll gie ye a wee hurl doon in ma motor.
I will transport you there in my car.

A'm jist gauny nick doon tae the pub furra quick wan.
I'm off to the pub, but I won't be drinking much.

Gauny shoot doon tae the papershoap an' git me fags?
Will you dash to the newsagents and purchase cigarettes for me?

THE BUSES ARE
AFF AN Ah
HUD TAE HUMPH
A' THIS
FAE THE
CENTRAL.

Ah'll no be long. A'm gauny see a man aboot a dug.
I'll return soon. Don't ask me where I'm going.

Ah hope ye'r no gaun oot gallavantin'.
I hope you'll not be wandering around and maybe getting into trouble.

Right, that's me, a'm away then!
I'll be taking my leave now!

The lift's oot the gemme an' ah hud tae sprachle up a' yon stairs.
The elevator is not operating and I had to climb the stairs.

That boat back fae Rossy wis mobbed, so it wis.
The boat returning from Rothesay was extremely crowded.

THE THINGS PEOPLE DO

If ah hiv tae pick, ah definately plump for that yin.
If I must choose, I certainly choose that one.

A' ye git fae politicians is body swerves.
Politicians are consistently evasive.

That dumplin's mad dug jist made a breenge at me for nuthin.
That idiot's dog attacked me for no reason.

There wis a heavy chap at the door.
There was a loud knock at the door.

Ye must be lousy wi' a' the clawin ye dae.
You must be infested with lice the way you continually scratch.

It must be aboot your turn noo tae crash the ash?
Is it not time for you to pass your cigarettes out?

Ur ye gauny stoap fuiterin aboot wi' that telly, you.
Why don't you stop interfering with the television.

He fair pit the hems oan that big back-kick and nae messin.
He certainly curtailed the activities of the defender with ease.

If there's a plump, we'll jist jook intae a shoap.
If it starts to rain, we'll take shelter in a shop.

Ah wis nae sooner in than ah wis papped back oot again.
I had hardly gained entry when I was ejected.

Mind an' no skail that jugga waater oan ma carpet.
Be careful not to spill water from that jug onto my carpet.

Ah'll jist go an' gie ma face a wee slunge.
I'll go and splash water on my face to freshen up.

Is that them away furra wee confab, then?
Is that them off for a little secret chat?

Wullye no staun still so's ye'll no cowp things.
Please stand still to avoid knocking things over.

PET LIKES AND HATES

If ye've got a jeely jaur, ye c'n come 'n catch baggy minnies.
If you have a jam jar, you can come and catch minnows.

Ah saw a wee speug swallyin a big blood sucker.
I saw a little sparrow swallowing a big worm.

Ma da's kept doos fur yonks.
My father has had pigeons for a very long time.

As ah wis walkin doon the road, ah saw a coo; a bull b'Goad.
As I walked along the road, I saw a cow; a bull, by God.

Yon wee dugs, wi' the big droopy lugs, are pure majic.
Those little dogs, with the big ears, are great.

There's a bum–bee's nest at the fitty oor gairden.
There's a bumble bee's nest at the bottom of our garden.

Ah canny staun yon jenny long legs 'cos they gie me the heeby-jeebies.
I really dislike those crane flies because they make my flesh crawl.

Ah shot a sparra wi' ma wee bow an' arra.
I shot a sparrow with my little bow and arrow.

Oor Maggie aye sings like a lintie at Hogmanay.
My sister Margaret always sings like a linnet on New Year's eve.

Ah mind yon prince when he wis still jist a puddock.
I remember that prince when he was just a frog.

Glesca's pure hoachin wi' stuckies.
Glasgow has a huge population of starlings.

Ah hate clappy doos but a c'n eat a punna wulks.
I hate mussels but I can eat lots of whelks.

Jookin aboot oan cuddies fair takes it oot oan ma bum.
Riding around on horses makes my bottom ache.

GLESCA'S PURE HOACHIN WI STUCKIES!

STOP PRESS

Jiner skelps wrang nail when he wanners his thumb.
Carpenter accidently hits his thumb with hammer.

Wummin droons dookin fur aipples.
Woman drowns trying to retrieve apples from bucket of
water with her teeth.

**Weather dizny know whit tae dae. Met man says he
plumps fur mair rain.**
Weather forecast uncertain. Spokesman for
Meteorological Office says he thinks it may rain again.

Faimily right in it efter cludgy goes oan the blink.
Family suffers when the plumbing in their toilet
breaks down.

**'Gers tae run patter classes so's a' thir foreign
players c'n tell whit the fans ur shouting aboot.**
Glasgow Rangers F.C. will organise language classes
for their English players who are having difficulty in
understanding the chants of the fans.

Hunners a thoosans a Glesca Phrase Books selt a'ready.
Many copies of the 'C'mon geeze yer patter' now sold.

Man gits wheeched inty jile fur skootin weed killer at Glesca's big flooer show.
Man goes to prison for spraying weed kiler at the Glasgow Garden Festival.

Boozers tae open a' hoors tae stoap the polis drinkin efter shuttin time.
Public houses to open 24 hours a day in bid to end after-hours drinking by police.

Lavvy divers strike causes a stink doon the toon.
Plumbers strike upsets people in Glasgow city centre.

Ten happy weans papped ooty school fur doggin' it.
Ten happy children are expelled from school for playing truant.

Man splashes oot when he tummles aff tap dale.
Man topples off high diving board at swimming pool.

Plane driver wis fleein at Glesca Airport.
Pilot drunk at Glasgow Airport.

Ginger lorry snaffled fae ootside the Co'.
Truck load of aerated water is stolen from outside
Co-operative store.

**Rammy breks oot when Jags git pit ooty peever
competition.**
Riot starts when Partick Thistle are beaten in
hopscotch competition.

Man wi' simit an gallowses lost in Troon.
Man with vest and braces blends into summer crowds
at Troon.

**Embra man tries tae coont buckets oan Clyde
sludge boat.**
Edinburgh man tries to count buckets on Clyde dredger.

INDEX TO SOME KEY WORDS.

N.B. ALL FIGURES IN INDEX REFER TO THE SECTION NUMBER.